INDONESIA

By Judy Thorpe and
Alicia Z. Klepeis

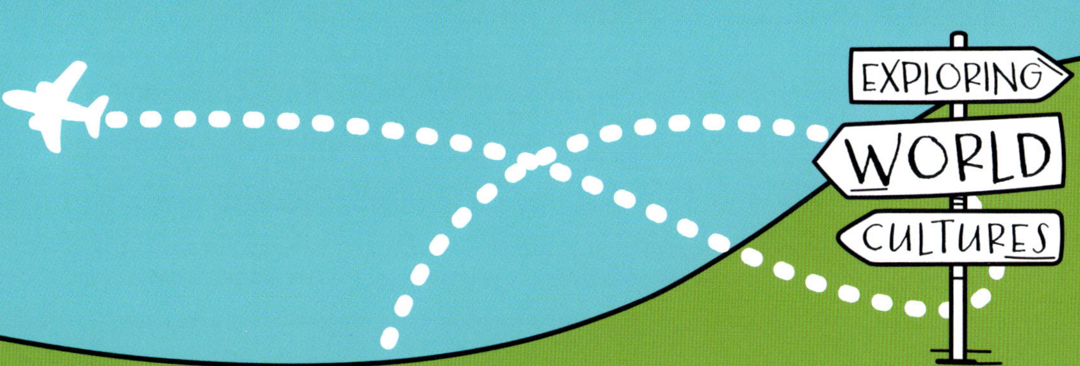

Published in 2025 by Cavendish Square Publishing, LLC
2544 Clinton Street, Buffalo, NY 14224

Second Edition

Website: cavendishsq.com

Library of Congress Cataloging-in-Publication Data

Names: Thorpe, Judy, author. | Klepeis, Alicia, 1971- author.
Title: Indonesia / Judy Thorpe and Alicia Z. Klepeis.
Description: Buffalo, NY : Cavendish Square Publishing, [2025] | Series: Exploring world cultures | Includes index.
Identifiers: LCCN 2024024636 | ISBN 9781502672971 (library binding) | ISBN 9781502672964 (paperback) | ISBN 9781502672988 (ebook)
Subjects: LCSH: Indonesia--Juvenile literature.
Classification: LCC DS615 .T464 2025 | DDC 959.8--dc23/eng/20240729
LC record available at https://lccn.loc.gov/2024024636

Writers: Alicia Z. Klepeis; Judy Thorpe (second edition)
Editor: Jennifer Lombardo
Copyeditors: Jill Keppeler and Danielle Haynes
Designer: Deanna Lepovich

The photographs in this book are used by permission and through the courtesy of: Cover, p. 21 Odua Images/Shutterstock.com; p. 4 fenkieandreas/Shutterstock.com; p. 5 Richard Whitcombe/Shutterstock.com; p. 6 Muslianshah Masrie/Shutterstock.com; p. 7 Peter Hermes Furian/Shutterstock.com; p. 8 Dimassakbr/Shutterstock.com; p. 9 World History Archive/Alamy Stock Photo; p. 10 Andreas H/Shutterstock.com; p. 11 riocontribae/Shutterstock.com; p. 12 Pepsco Studio/Shutterstock.com; p. 13 Surasak Saenjai/Shutterstock.com; p. 15 (top) Vitaly Titov/Shutterstock.com; p. 15 (bottom) Darren Kurnia/Shutterstock.com; p. 16 Lambang Ariyadi/Shutterstock.com; p. 17 PhotopankPL/Shutterstock.com; p. 18 Humba Frame/Shutterstock.com; p. 19 Evans Winanda Wirga/Shutterstock.com; p. 20 Guitar photographer/Shutterstock.com; p. 22 Maslan12/Shutterstock.com; p. 23 Javanese script01/Wikimedia Commons; p. 24 (main) Pikul Noorod/Shutterstock.com; p. 24 (inset) Jaya Tri Hartono/Shutterstock.com; p. 25 raditya/Shutterstock.com; p. 26 Mo Wu/Shutterstock.com; p. 27 HEGEDARIA/Shutterstock.com; p. 28 Hanif Setia/Shutterstock.com; p. 29 Ariyani Tedjo/Shutterstock.com.

CPSIA compliance information: Batch #CW25CSQ: For further information contact Cavendish Square Publishing LLC at 1-877-980-4450.

Printed in the United States of America

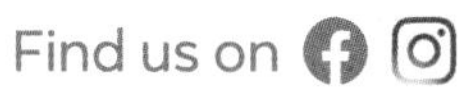

CONTENTS

Introduction 4

Chapter 1 Geography 6

Chapter 2 History 8

Chapter 3 Government 10

Chapter 4 The Economy 12

Chapter 5 The Environment 14

Chapter 6 The People Today 16

Chapter 7 Lifestyle 18

Chapter 8 Religion 20

Chapter 9 Language 22

Chapter 10 Arts and Festivals 24

Chapter 11 Fun and Play 26

Chapter 12 Food 28

Glossary 30

Find Out More 31

Index 32

INTRODUCTION

Indonesia is an Asian country that is made up of more than 17,000 islands. The first Indonesian civilization was founded around 1000 BCE. Starting in 1512 CE, different groups of Europeans arrived on the islands. They controlled Indonesia for many years. The country won its independence in 1949. More than 275 million people live there today.

Indonesia has many beautiful places to visit. There are lakes, mountains, coral reefs, and caves. Tourists, or visitors, come from around the world to see Indonesia's beaches and rainforests. They also come to scuba dive or visit the country's ancient temples.

Scuba divers use tanks of air that let them stay underwater for long periods of time.

Indonesia has a very **unique** culture, or way of life. Its art, music, and dance styles are ancient, or very old. However, Indonesians also enjoy playing sports, going to the mall, and watching TV, just like people in other parts of the world today.

Like all countries, Indonesia has its problems. For example, **climate change** is making sea levels rise everywhere in the world. In Indonesia, this is causing widespread flooding. The government has promised to make changes, but little has been done as of 2024.

People only live on about 6,000 of Indonesia's islands. Shown here is the tiny island of Gili Air, which is surrounded by a beach and a coral reef.

GEOGRAPHY

The Indonesian archipelago, or group of islands, covers 735,358 square miles (1,904,569 square kilometers). Indonesia is bordered by the countries of Malaysia, Papua New Guinea, and Timor-Leste.

Some of Indonesia's larger islands have mountains. Puncak Jaya, on the island of New Guinea, is 16,024 feet (4,884 meters) tall. It is the tallest point in Indonesia as well as the tallest mountain on any island in the world.

FACT!

If all of Indonesia's islands were pushed together into one landmass, it would be three times the size of Texas.

Many of Indonesia's islands are so small they do not appear on maps.

Indonesia is part of the Ring of Fire. This is a horseshoe-shaped chain of volcanoes around the edge of the Pacific Ocean. Indonesia has more active volcanoes than any other country on Earth.

The island of Borneo is split among three countries. Kalimantan, the Indonesian part, covers two-thirds of the island. The tiny country of Brunei makes up about 1 percent of the island. Malaysia controls the rest.

MAIN ISLANDS

Most of Indonesia's population lives on five main islands. These are Sumatra, Java, Kalimantan, Sulawesi, and Papua. Papua covers half of the world's second-largest island, New Guinea. The other half is the independent country of Papua New Guinea.

HISTORY

Early Indonesia was made up of many kingdoms. Because the islands in the archipelago were so scattered, many different cultures formed within the area.

FACT!

Under Dutch rule, Indonesia was known as the Netherlands (or Dutch) East Indies.

In 1512, **colonizers** arrived from Portugal looking for spices. They controlled parts of Indonesia until the 1600s. Then, the Dutch took power. They ruled parts of Indonesia until World War II (1939–1945). Japan took over Indonesia from 1942 to 1945.

This building in Jakarta, Indonesia, was the office of the governor during Dutch colonial rule. The sign says "Governor's Office" in Dutch.

Indonesia declared independence in August 1945, but it was not accepted by the rest of the world until 1949. A man named General Suharto became president in 1967. He ruled the country as a military **dictator** until 1998. Today, Indonesians vote for their leaders.

This drawing shows what Java man may have looked like.

JAVA MAN

In 1891, some bones of an **extinct** species, or type, of human were uncovered on the island of Java. Both this species and this person became known as "Java man." Java man showed that humans had been living in Indonesia for more than 1 million years.

GOVERNMENT

Indonesia is split into 38 parts called provinces. There is only one national capital district, or area. The capital of Indonesia is Jakarta.

Jakarta has many modern buildings.

FEARS FOR THE FUTURE

In 2024, Prabowo Subianto won Indonesia's presidential election. However, people both in and outside of Indonesia are worried about this. Prabowo hurt many people while he was in the military under Suharto's rule. People are unsure whether he will do this again as president.

Indonesia's government has three parts, or branches: legislative, judicial, and executive. In Indonesia, part of the legislative branch is called the House of Representatives. It makes the laws. The Regional Representative Council also forms part of the legislative branch. It does not directly make laws.

The judicial branch tells people what the laws mean. It includes Indonesia's courts. The executive branch makes sure people follow the laws. It includes the president, their cabinet, and the vice president. Joko Widodo, Indonesia's seventh president, served from 2014 to 2024.

FACT!

Indonesians have a nickname for Joko Widodo. They call him "Jokowi."

Prabowo Subianto won the 2024 presidential election in Indonesia.

THE ECONOMY

Indonesia has a very strong **economy**. Its main exports, or items it sells to other countries, include oil, gas, palm oil, cars, and rubber. The country's most important trading partners include China, Japan, Singapore, South Korea, and the United States.

Almost half of Indonesian workers have service jobs. Some work in restaurants, banks, or hotels. Others work in national parks, hospitals, or stores. **Tourism** is a big part of the economy.

FACT!

One U.S. dollar is equal to about 16,000 rupiah.

Indonesia's money is called the rupiah.

Because Indonesia is surrounded by water, fishing is an important job. Farming is also important. Indonesian farmers grow crops such as coffee, cocoa, and spices. Miners dig for minerals like copper and tin. Indonesia also has the world's largest supply of nickel.

Indonesia is the world's second-largest producer of natural rubber. Rubber is made from the sap of the rubber tree. Indonesians collect the sap like this.

DOMESTIC VS. INTERNATIONAL

Much of Indonesia's money comes from domestic sources. This means other Indonesians are the main buyers of the things the country makes. International trade accounts for only 20 percent of Indonesia's economy. This is lower than most other Asian countries.

THE ENVIRONMENT

Indonesia is home to many kinds of animals. More than 100 of them are endangered, or close to dying out. Indonesia is facing environmental issues that make this problem worse. For example, huge areas of rainforest are cut down every year to make room for farmland, new buildings, and tourist sites. Many plants and animals are dying out because of this.

The capital city of Jakarta has bad air pollution from cars and factories. Water pollution is another big problem. Many people do not have clean water to drink or wash with. Polluted water can make people and animals sick.

KEEPING NATURE SAFE

Indonesia makes up only 1 percent of Earth's land. However, its rainforests contain 10 percent of the world's plant species, 12 percent of all **mammal** species, and 17 percent of all bird species. To protect these plants and animals, or keep them safe, the government has passed new laws limiting how land can be used.

The tarsier is one of the world's smallest **primates**. It is native to Indonesia.

FACT!

In 2024, more than 40,000 families were killed, hurt, or made homeless by major floods and landslides on Sumatra. Experts say natural **disasters** are getting worse due to climate change.

The world's largest flower, the corpse flower, can be found in Indonesia's rainforests. It gets its name from its terrible smell, which people say is similar to that of a dead body.

THE PEOPLE TODAY

There are more than 1,300 Indonesian **ethnic** groups. The Javanese people are the largest group. They make up 40 percent of Indonesians. The Javanese mainly live in the eastern and central agricultural, or farming, areas on Java.

This bride and groom are wearing ***traditional*** *Javanese wedding clothing.*

A DIVERSE COUNTRY

With so many different ethnic groups, Indonesia is one of the world's most ethnically diverse, or different, countries. Indonesia's motto, or official saying, is "Unity in Diversity." This shows that although the groups have different cultures, they are all connected as Indonesians.

Indonesia's second-largest group is the Sundanese people. They make up about 16 percent. The Sundanese people live mostly in the western part of Java. The rest of the Indonesian population is split among hundreds of smaller ethnic groups.

Indonesia's ethnic groups often have their own unique cultures. These include their music, arts, **celebrations**, and even jobs. For example, the Bugis and Makassarese people of Sulawesi are known for making boats.

FACT!
Indonesia is the fourth-most populated country in the world.

The Dayak people live on the island of Borneo. They have traditionally lived in longhouses similar to this one. Today, many Dayak people work on palm oil plantations or in timber camps.

LIFESTYLE

Because Indonesia is a collection of cultures and islands, lifestyles are different depending on which part of the country someone lives in. About half of all Indonesians live in cities. There, life is much the same as in any large city on Earth.

FACT!
Building and flying kites is a popular activity for Indonesians, especially teens.

Whether they live in the city or the country, one thing that unites many Indonesians is their love for family.

People in the city might walk, ride a bike, or take a bus to work. They often have cell phones. Some also own televisions.

People in Indonesia's countryside often live simply. Not everyone has electricity. Some people grow crops. Others work in the mines. People in the country have less **access** to places such as hospitals and schools.

A BIG GAP

The wealth gap in Indonesia is the sixth largest in the world. The four richest Indonesian men have more wealth than the 100 million poorest people.

About half of Indonesian women have jobs. One popular job for women is making crafts to sell to tourists or other Indonesians.

RELIGION

Indonesia is the world's largest Muslim country. Islam spread to the country around the end of the 1300s. About 87 percent of the people today are Muslim. Another 11 percent are Christian–either Protestant or Catholic. Indonesia also has small Buddhist, Hindu, and Confucian populations.

FACT!

Most Indonesians say the diversity of religions, or faiths, makes their country stronger.

Before Islam spread to Indonesia, most Indonesians were Hindu or Buddhist. Many old temples, such as this Hindu temple in Bali, can still be seen around the islands.

Muslim services are held in buildings called mosques. There, men and women pray separately. Indonesian Muslims honor sacred, or holy, times such as Ramadan. During Ramadan, Muslims do not eat or drink while the sun is up. At the end of this holy month, there is a large festival, or celebration, called Eid al-Fitr.

Many Muslim women cover their arms, legs, and heads.

FORCED TO CHOOSE

Indonesia has six official religions. People must choose one to list on their government identity card. Choosing no religion is not allowed.

LANGUAGE

A country's official language is the one used in government, schools, and businesses. Indonesia's official language is Bahasa Indonesia. More than 200 million people around the world speak this language. Unlike many other Asian languages, Bahasa Indonesia uses the same alphabet as English.

Most Indonesian newspapers are written in Bahasa Indonesia. It is also possible to find newspapers in English and Chinese.

FACT!

More than 700 different languages are spoken in Indonesia.

When Indonesia was trying to gain its independence from the Netherlands, most people spoke Malay. A group of Indonesians changed Malay to create Bahasa Indonesia. The idea was that now all Indonesians would be able to communicate with each other. It also meant that no ethnic group's language would be made more important than the others. However, many Indonesians today don't like Bahasa Indonesia and don't often speak it unless they have to.

ETHNIC LANGUAGES

Most people grow up learning the language of their ethnic group. They learn Bahasa Indonesia as a second language in school. Many Indonesians see themselves as their ethnicity first and Indonesian second.

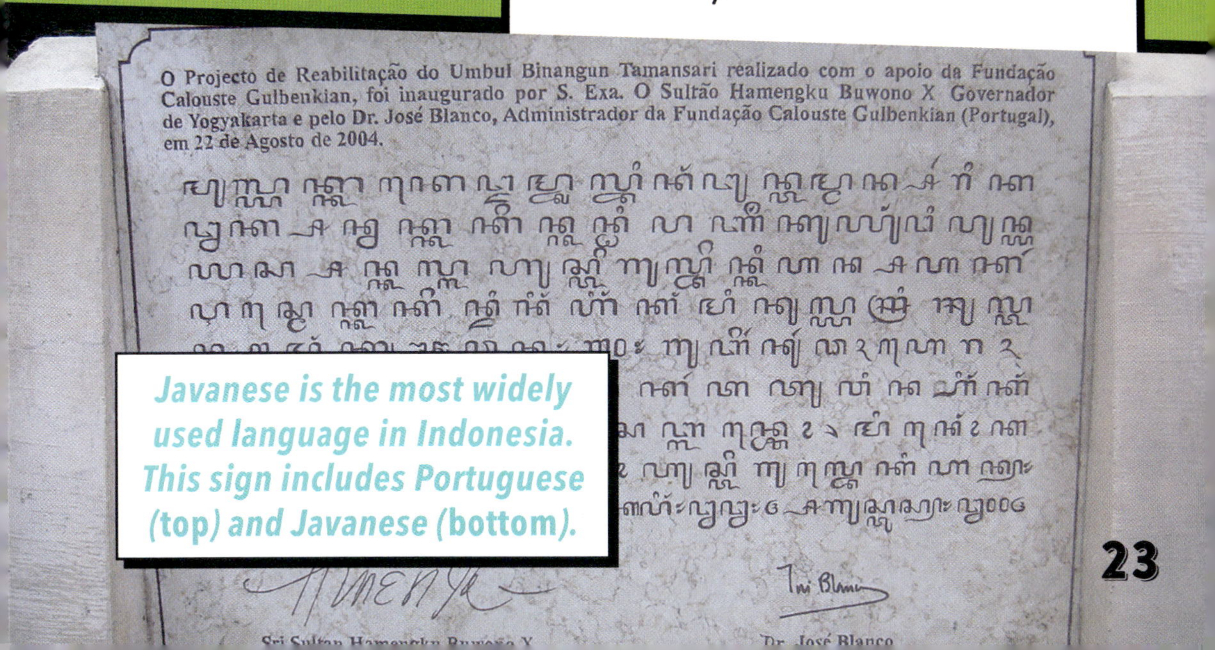

Javanese is the most widely used language in Indonesia. This sign includes Portuguese (top) and Javanese (bottom).

ARTS AND FESTIVALS

Indonesian art has many unique styles. As the Javanese are the largest ethnic group, their style is best known around the world, especially their detailed shadow puppets and fabrics.

FACT!

Two museums in Jakarta show off many examples of Indonesia's artworks.

Many Indonesians enjoy watching shadow puppet performances. Shadow puppetry has been practiced in several Asian cultures since ancient times.

Indonesia is famous for a type of cloth called batik. Batik artists create designs on cloth using wax and dye.

Dance and music are two other important art forms in Indonesia. The island of Bali is known worldwide for its unique dance performances.

Indonesians celebrate many festivals throughout the year. Some are religious. Others focus on the arts. Some celebrations are regional, or only held in certain parts of the country. For example, a week-long festival is held each summer on the island of Samosir. The festival includes food, music, and boxing matches.

FULL MOON FESTIVALS

Each month when the moon is full, Indonesians—especially in Bali—hold a special festival. They honor the moon god, Chandra, by dressing up in special clothing and bringing offerings of food and flowers to local temples.

FUN AND PLAY

What people do for fun in Indonesia depends a lot on where they live and what the local culture is. Soccer and badminton are two of the most popular sports in Indonesia. Basketball and boxing are commonly watched and played as well. To relax, many Indonesians enjoy fishing and swimming at the beach.

CAT AND MOUSE

An Indonesian game called *kucing-kucingan* ("cat and mouse") has existed in Java since at least 1913. Players decide who will be the cat and who will be the mouse. Everyone who has not been chosen holds hands in a circle to try to protect the mouse from the cat.

Komodo National Park is especially popular with tourists because it's home to the largest lizard on Earth: the Komodo dragon.

Art and music are important parts of Indonesian culture. Many Indonesians enjoy watching a shadow puppet show, going to a dance, or playing music with friends and family.

Many Indonesians also like to play games. Some, such as hide and seek— called *petak umpet* in Indonesia—are common all over the world. Others are unique to Indonesia.

FACT!
Video games are very popular in Indonesia, especially among people who live in cities.

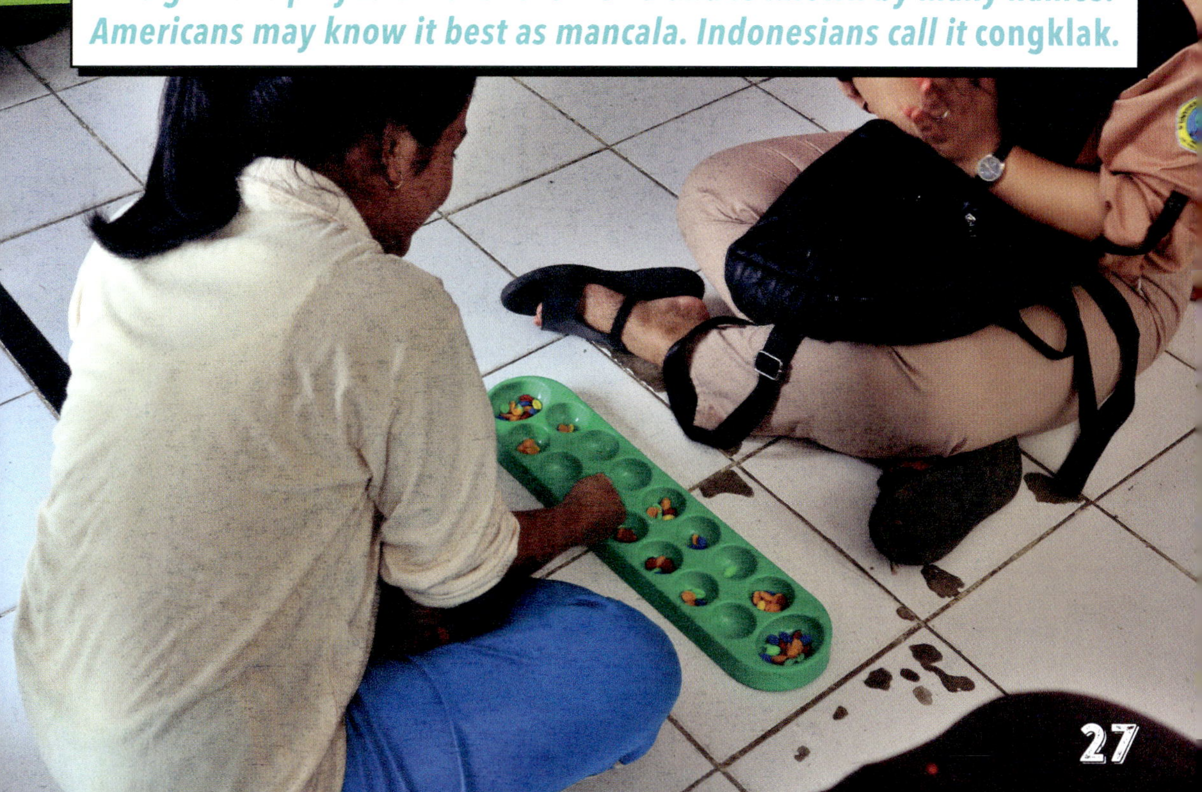

This game is played all over the world and is known by many names. Americans may know it best as mancala. Indonesians call it congklak.

FOOD

Indonesians use many spices such as chili and cumin in their dishes. Coconut milk is commonly used as well.

People in Indonesia eat a lot of seafood. Meat skewers known as satay are also popular. To make satay, chicken, goat, and other meats are put on a skewer, or stick. The skewered meats are grilled and then served with peanut sauce.

Es teler ***is a popular Indonesian dessert. Shaved ice is topped with avocado, coconut meat, and jackfruit.***

Many people consider *nasi goreng* to be Indonesia's national dish. It is a fried rice dish that often contains meat and vegetables. It can be eaten with breakfast, lunch, and dinner.

FACT!

Rice is a staple of Indonesian cooking. It's the main part of most dishes.

Indonesians eat a wide variety of delicious foods.

THE SPICE ISLANDS

More than half of the spices people use every day were first grown in Indonesia. These include nutmeg, cloves, pepper, and cinnamon. The country still grows and exports many of the world's spices.

GLOSSARY

access: The freedom or ability to get or make use of something.

celebration: A time to show happiness for an event through activities such as eating or playing music.

climate change: Long-term change in Earth's climate, or weather over a long period of time, caused mainly by human activities such as burning oil and natural gas.

colonizer: A person who moves to a new place to live on land that was taken from Indigenous peoples.

dictator: Someone who rules a country by force.

disaster: An event that causes much suffering or loss.

economy: The way goods and services are made and sold.

ethnic: Relating to groups of people with common traits and customs and a sense of shared identity.

extinct: No longer living.

mammal: A warm-blooded animal that has a backbone and hair, breathes air, and feeds milk to its young.

primate: Any animal from the group that includes humans, apes, and monkeys.

tourism: The business of drawing in tourists, or people traveling to visit another place.

traditional: Having to do with long-practiced customs.

unique: Special, or one of a kind.

FIND OUT MORE

Books

Anderson, Shannon. *Indonesia*. Minneapolis, MN: Bellwether Media, 2024.

Barghoorn, Linda. *Focus on Indonesia*. St. Catharines, ON: Crabtree Publishing, 2024.

Low, Yvonne Yanmei. *Awesome Art Indonesia: 10 Works from the Archipelago Everyone Should Know*. Singapore: National Gallery Singapore, 2020.

Websites

Globe Trottin' Kids: Indonesia
www.globetrottinkids.com/indonesia
Take a look through this website's amazing photo gallery.

Kiddle: Indonesia Facts for Kids
kids.kiddle.co/Indonesia
Read more about Indonesia's past and present.

Video

YouTube: Let's Take a Journey: Indonesia!
www.youtube.com/watch?v=PcOsgbWHv7Y
In this video from Miacademy Learning Channel, Justin learns about what life is like for Indonesian kids.

Publisher's note to educators and parents: Our editors have carefully reviewed these websites to ensure that they are suitable for students. Many websites change frequently, however, and we cannot guarantee that a site's future contents will continue to meet our high standards of quality and educational value. Be advised that students should be closely supervised whenever they access the internet.

INDEX

A
agriculture, 13, 16, 17, 19
art, 5, 17, 24, 25, 27

C
climate change, 15
colonization, 8
cuisine/food, 25, 28, 29

D
dance, 5, 25, 27

E
economy, 12, 13
ethnicity, 16, 17, 23, 24

F
flora/plants, 4, 14, 15

G
government, 9, 10, 11, 14

J
Japan, 8
Java, 7, 9, 16, 17
Joko Widodo, 11

K
Kalimantan/Borneo, 7, 17

L
lakes, 4
language, 22, 23

M
mining, 13, 19
mountains, 4, 6
music, 5, 17, 25, 27

P
Papua, 7
Prabowo Subianto, 10, 11

R
religion, 4, 20, 21, 25

S
sports, 5, 26
Suharto (president), 9
Sumatra, 7

V
volcanoes, 7

W
wildlife, 14, 15, 26